Life's
Extras

Life's Extras

ARCHIBALD RUTLEDGE

This edition is published
to commemorate the one-
hundredth anniversary of the
birth of Archibald Rutledge at
McClellanville, South Carolina,
October 23, 1883

SANDLAPPER PUBLISHING CO., INC.
Orangeburg, South Carolina 1983

The publisher is grateful to Fleming H. Revell Company for the right to publish their 1928 edition of "Life's Extras."

Grateful acknowledgement is also made to Judge Irvine H. Rutledge for his permission to reprint the following Archibald Rutledge works: "When the Yankee Band Played Dixie" from *We Called Him Flintlock*, "Sam Singleton, Boatman" from *It Will Be Daybreak Soon*, and the poems, "The Compass" and "A Song of Hope."

ISBN 0-87844-055-0

Published by Sandlapper Publishing Co., Inc.
P.O. Box 1932
Orangeburg, South Carolina 29116-1932
Designed by Design for Publishing, Bob Nance
Illustrated by Robin Nance

Manufactured in the United States of America

Contents

Introduction

Until I was nine or ten, I thought of my father, Archibald Rutledge, only as a wonderful, interesting, loving father. The family consisted of my parents, my two older brothers, and me. Our large house in Mercersburg, Pennsylvania, was always full to overflowing with guns, fishing rods, baseball equipment, and other impediments such as would have driven a less patient and loving mother up a wall.

A large garage and yard served to house rabbits, pigeons, guinea pigs, birds, dogs, cats, bantam chickens, deer hounds, and a goat named Gunga Din. My father always kept a big garden, and my brothers and

I had a small business each summer of selling produce from this garden from a small wagon which Gunga Din pulled patiently around the neighborhood. On my first trip around town, at age five, my brothers nearly kicked me off the team when I ate all the strawberries we had taken with us to sell.

By the age of nine or ten I made an important discovery: my father wrote books about his boyhood at Hampton Plantation in South Carolina. He taught and wrote to support his family. The first of his books that I read was *Old Plantation Days*, published some years before I was born. From it I learned of deer, wild turkeys, alligators, foxes, moccasins, and the great flocks of bobolinks, or rice birds, that came to feast on the annual rice crop. I learned about his black comrades—Scipio, Galboa, Prince, and Gabriel— long before I grew up to enjoy many a happy day in the woods with my father, my brothers, Prince, Gabriel and Prince's three sons.

In Mercersburg our house sat next to a pretty woods. Each morning my father would go there to a chair with an arm on it for writing and would sit for two hours writing until the family was up and organized. After breakfast he would go teach classes in senior English at Mercersburg Academy. After his last class in the afternoon, we would all go to work in the garden, or go trout fishing or arrowhead hunting; or in the autumn, we would take our bird dog out for quail.

As I entered college, a series of articles by my father which appeared in the *American Magazine* brought him wide acclaim. One of these called "Life's Extras" was made into a small book published by Fleming Revell in 1928. It became an instant success and has gone through eleven or twelve printings, selling over a million copies. This little book represents my father at his best and illustrates his love of nature, his deep faith, and his spiritual vision.

Recently, the whole Rutledge clan learned with the greatest pleasure that the SANDLAPPER planned to publish a new edition of *Life's Extras* on the one hundredth anniversary of my father's birthday, October 23, 1883. This news was especially pleasing because for some time the SANDLAPPER has been republishing what is probably my father's most popular book, *Home by the River*, the story of his life at Hampton Plantation.

Irvine H. Rutledge.

April 30, 1983

Life's Extras

My casual acquaintance on the train that was speeding across the autumn landscape seemed thoughtful, reflective, a little wistful as we talked about the things we saw from the car window. At last we came to a big meadow wherein were grazing half a hundred beef cattle. I said something inane about the prosperity of the country, the glowing future of the live-stock industry, and so forth. "Look at those little daisies," he said, pointing to a bright patch of them in a far corner of the meadow. Then he added, "Cattle somehow can't thrill me. There's more hope for humanity in a wild flower than in tons of beef."

3

Long after he left me, I kept thinking of what he had said, wondering just what he had meant. His idea, of course, was that a wild flower is one of life's extras, one of those things that we do not *have* to have but which we enjoy all the more for that very reason.

The more I thought about this, the more it appeared that Creation supplies us with only two kinds of things: necessities and extras. Sunlight, air, water, food, shelter—these are among the bare necessities. With them we can exist. But moonlight and starlight are distinctly extras; so are music, the perfumes, flowers. The wind is perhaps a necessity; but the song that it croons through the morning pines is a different thing.

The fascinating part about all this is not the tabulating of life's necessities and life's extras; it is rather the question, Who put them here, and for what purpose? Furthermore, shall we not find, through some stories of personal experience, that the curious and significant remark of my casual acquaintance was right? I do not presume that my actual living this mortal life has in any way been unique, especially as regards this matter of life's extras; yet, if I can tell what they have meant to me, I shall perhaps be voicing the experience and the hope of many.

I remember one October night visiting a friend who was lying very sick. There was a full moon that night; and as I walked down the village street on my sad mission I felt the silvery beauty of it quiet my heart. The world lay lustrous. There was no scrawny bush nor ugly clod that was not transfigured in that glory. A little breeze over the brimming salt tide brought aromatic marshy odors. It seemed to me that some power was trying to make beauty take away my sadness. I found my friend not less aware than I was of the beauty of the night. He could look from his window and see the argent glamour of it all: how it flooded the gleaming tide with celestial lights; how it ran long white lances through the swarthy cedars; how it tinged with soft radiance the locusts and the mimosas. He felt the breeze too, and delighted in the odours that it brought of the happy world beyond his window.

As I sat beside him, a mocking bird began to sing in the moonlight, chanting divinely. I know the song reached our spirits. On the table by the bed were all the necessities for a sick man; but he had small comfort from them. But the moonlight, and the hale fragrances, and the wild song of the bird—these brought peace to his heart.

Long afterward he said to me, "Do you remember that night? I thought it would be my last. But from the time the birdsong came through that window I felt that I would get well. I don't talk much about these things, but I felt that all that beauty and peace were really the love of God. I guess He does not love us with words: He loves us by giving us everything we need—in every way."

It must be as he said.

At any rate, I know that a thoughtful consideration of life's extras has done more to give my faith in God actual conviction than all the sermons I ever heard. My knowledge of theology is hardly more ample than that of a bushman of Borneo; but I am absolutely unshaken in my faith that God created us, loves us, and wants us not only to be good but to be happy. He ministers to our bodies by the necessities that abound in the world; and to our spirits by the beauty that adorns creation. One has no difficulty in discovering, in the vast scheme of things, an extraordinary, an exciting, provision and prevision. As philosophy, I know not if this will stand; but I do know that a belief in it has brought me close to God.

I cannot regard the "fiery funeral of foliage old" as accidental, nor the gorgeous pageantry of sunset as anything but the manifestation of divine art. I stood recently on the shores of a mountain lake at sundown after a heavy rain, and watched for an hour the magnificence of the west; the huge clouds smoldering, the long lanes of emerald light between them, then isolated clouds like red roses climbing up some oriel window of the sky, the deep refulgence behind it all. Superb as it was, momently it changed, so that I saw in reality a score of sunsets. I looked across the lonely, limpid lake, past the dark forest, far into the heart of the flaming, fading skies. I was sure that God had done that; moreover, that He had done it for a purpose. When did He ever do anything idly? And what was the purpose? Surely to fill the hearts of His children with a sense of beauty and of awe, and to teach them of His loving care.

Neither a day-dawning nor a sunset (with all its attendant beauty) is really a necessity. It is one of life's extras. It is a visit to an incomparable art gallery; and no one has to pay any admission fee. The human mind, being somewhat proud and perverse, may be inclined to reject this kind of proof of God's love. But the human heart can hardly do so. And in things spiritual I do not know but that the heart is by far the better guide.

Not long ago, I visited a lonely cabin in the North Carolina mountains, whence the owner had just been taken, charged with murder. He and a neighbor had had a fatal altercation about a line fence, and he had "drawn" more quickly than the other. The accused had borne a good reputation up to this time. Both men had seen service in France. I was rather well acquainted with both families.

As I went up the old gullied mountain road toward the home of the first, I noticed in the wild glen, down which a white stream gurgled and spurted, incessant, vehement, and joyous, that the rhododendrons were in blossom. There may be a more beautiful flower, but I have not seen it—taking it all in all, and considering the wildwood setting in which it invariably grows. To look at this wondrous flower and not to feel that God exquisitely designed it, and did it not merely as a vagrant artist but with precision and nobility of purpose is to me incredible. Ere long I reached the cabin, and one of the man's sisters greeted me and talked with me. Over the humble mantel I saw a crude little photograph of him in his uniform; and beside it, in a small bottle that functioned as a vase, I saw a sprig of rhododendron blossom. I looked at the picture; then I said something casual about the flower.

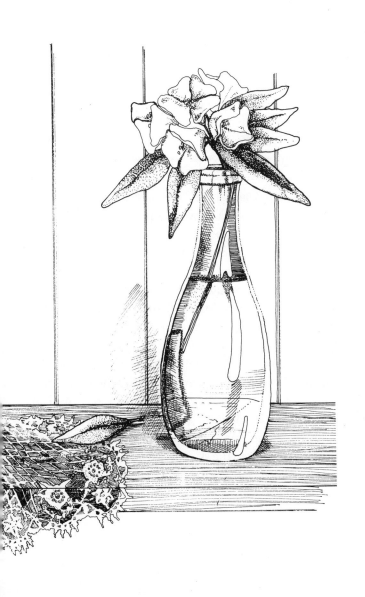

"I don't know why," my hostess said, "but to have it there helps me. It 'minds me of God."

I have always loved the eloquence of simple people. What they say, coming from the heart, often goes straight to the heart. "It 'minds me of God." I never see a rhododendron without remembering that. And are not all of life's extras reminders of the love and the yearning compassion of God?

I mentioned sunsets and sunrises as extras. Almost the whole complex and wonderful matter of color in the world seems as extra. The color of the sky might have been a dingy gray, or a painful yellow, or a plum-colored purple. But it is sapphire; and my philosophy makes me believe that such a color for the sky is by no means the result of mere chance. Granted that it is the result of the operation of certain laws, forces, and conditions; yet behind it all, back of the realized dream, is the mighty intelligence of the Creator, the vast amplitude of the dreamer's comprehension. And let us not forget that the two colors at which we can gaze longest are blue and green. There is about them a coolness, a serenity, a spirit of fragrant peace. And as the blue prevails in the sky, the green does upon earth.

I have often heard people say that they would like to remake the world. Well, I am glad that we don't have to live in a man-made world. If we consider merely the least of the marvelous provisions for our comfort and our happiness, we can realize how impossible would be an earth and a scheme of life that man had made. And we should feel, also, that David was right: "For as the heaven is high above the earth, so great is His mercy toward them that fear Him." How high is the heaven? Illimitable. And so is God's love.

To a sophisticated person, this sort of belief may seem too childlike. Yet I have the gravest suspicions of sophistication. I have never discovered it in nature; and to me it seems that instead of being a proof of enlightenment and culture, it is the evidence rather of ignorance, and perhaps of folly. It is the triumph of shallowness and sterility. The real trouble with a sophisticated person is not that he knows too much, but that he knows too little.

Probably everyone has had some kind of experience with a star, or with the stars. I mean that, at some moment, a star has risen, or has been seen, or has set amid circumstances that made the memory of it a part of one's life. I remember that the morning star I used to see blazing above the plantation pines, when I was up early to feed the stock, or to be about some other work, used to thrill me with the beauty of its startling radiance. It seemed all dewy and throbbing—a thing alive, glorious and immortal. God set it there, I felt, as a reminder of His presence, so that we might begin our day with the thought of Him. So when the evening came, a great beacon of the twilight reminds us of Him again. Our days and nights are sentineled by the splendid warders of God.

I once had a curious experience with a star. I was driving home to the plantation, in the old motorless days, when I was overtaken at dusk by a storm of hurricane violence. Inky darkness shrouded the world. I could not even see the road ahead or behind. The thunder and lightning were appalling. Finally, a bolt struck a pine not twenty feet from my buggy. My horse had stood a good deal from this storm; but now he made a sudden dash. He broke away through the forest, and I could not hold him. In a moment he had run between two pines standing close together, had smashed both shafts, and had torn loose from the buggy and from me. Into the howling darkness he vanished.

The rain came down as if it meant to make a joke of the Flood. The thunder blared. The lightning became most uncomfortably intimate and intrusive. I heard near me great trees go crashing down in the fury of the tempest. Alone I was, defenseless, in profound darkness. I knew in a way where I was, and to locate myself the better I looked toward what I believed to be the west.

Through the heavy arras of the rain, to my amazement, I saw a little rift in the storm-rack, hardly bigger than my hand, in the very heart of which the evening star gleamed in dewy-silver solitude. In all the stillness of felicity it shone serenely, saying to my heart, "This storm is an impostor. It is momentary. The sky is here, and the stars; all shall be well."

Amid all the desolation about me, and the seemingly hopeless chaos, here came a celestial message. Shining through the storm-rack, its light reminded me of something past our world. Taking heart, I waded out to the road, found my horse waiting for me half a mile down its gleaming length, rode homeward through the breaking storm, and reached the house in full, calm starlight. Stars fill me with a sense of God; and the heart cannot help being grateful when it remembers that the beauty and the wonder of them may be accounted things not to enable us to exist, but gifts of love to make us joyous.

If there is anything in life in which I take a pardonable pride, it is in my friendship for certain old woodsmen and hunters; obscure men, as far as the world is concerned, but faithful friends, loyal comrades. Occasionally one will tell me something intimate about himself; and when he does it is usually remarkable, as I believe the following story is. I shall give it without embellishment.

"It happened last June," my friend told me, as we

were sitting together on a pine log in the depths of a virgin forest. "I tell it to you because I know if you tell it, you will never use my name. Bill Moore and I, you see, had had trouble between us for years. The last time we met in town, if friends hadn't separated us we would have finished the thing right there. A lot of things had made us feel as we did; and everything that happened appeared to make it worse.

"After that night in town, I figured that one of us would get the other. I knew he always carried a gun, and I began to do the same. Well, that day in June one of the field hands told me that Bill said he would get me. I made up my mind to meet him a little more than halfway, and late that afternoon I rode up toward Bill's house, about three miles from mine, intending to have the thing over. A man can't live in that kind of suspense.

"A mile from his house, I saw somebody coming down the road. The man was riding too, and he looked like Bill. I just turned off the road into one of these here bay-branches, where I would be hid well. There I sat still on my horse, with the bushes all around me, and with my hand on my gun and the devil in my heart. I put up my left hand to pull aside a little limb, when on it I saw a white flower, a sweet bay flower. And I smelt it, too. My mother used to love that flower; and when I was a boy she made me bring a bush from the swamp and plant it in the yard for her. She was buried with one of them same white flowers in her hand. And, you know, I forgot all about why I had come down that road.

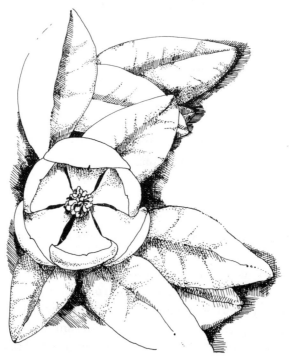

"You'll think I was a fool, but that flower set me to thinking about my mother, and about them old days, and about the kind of man she hoped I might be when she was gone. The first thing I knew the man on horseback was right opposite me in the road. And it was Bill, all right.

"But in the few minutes he had taken to come up, something had happened to me. I didn't want to harm him now. I didn't feel that I had to look out for myself. Perhaps I did a risky thing, but I rode out of the bushes, calling to him. Something in the way I came up made him know it was all right. And it was all right, 'cause we made it right there and then; and we are better friends than ever we were before anything happened. Now what do you think of that—and all because of a little white flower? But it's all the truth, just as I'm telling you."

He "redeemeth thy life from destruction," says the Psalmist; but we do not often think of the deft and beautiful ways in which God works. Beauty is made to touch the heart, a right spirit is renewed, and the life is redeemed. I don't think this is preaching; I hope not, for of all men I am the least capable or worthy to undertake that. It just seems to me like a rehearsal of truth. Surely life's extras not only give us happiness in a positive way but also indirectly: by saving us from the tragic loss of our nobler instincts, they rescue us in times of peril.

There are very few sounds in the natural world that are harsh. Even the massive rolling of thunder has about it something of solemn beauty. In anthems the sea rolls on the beach; and in the sunny shallows there are water-harps forever making melodies. The wind is a chorister. Many a wild bird can warble like an aerial rivulet. (The world is really a melodious place, full of soft sounds and harmony. Man makes it riotous and blatant.)

I remember being especially impressed with this truth when I went one day into the forest to try to escape from a grief that had come to me—the loss of one dearly beloved.

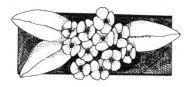

A little way within the borders of that fragrant, dewy forest, where giant yellow pines, tall as the masts of brigantines and full of dim contralto music in their crowns, rejoiced in the sunshine—just here I heard a parula-warbler singing. He was in the crest of a bald cypress, high over the dreamy waters of a little woodland lake. The bird's song sounded like a delicate astral flute, sounded softly and sweetly, to lure me out of my trouble. High in the heavenly blue this chorister was, joyous in that halcyon repose that the heart enjoys when it is at peace. Like a voice of a spirit was this music; it came to me calmly yet thrillingly. Like a quieting hand was that beautiful song, to cool the fever of care, to still the pulse's leap.

All about me were the rejoicing looks of the flowers, and the shining hush and loveliness of dew-hung ferns and bushes, and the gentle, pure passion of the sunlight. And music there was from myriads of sources: gossamer lyrics from bees; the laughter of a little stream jesting with the roots of a mighty pine. The wind's soft wand touched the tall grasses and the sweet myrtles into a sibilant elfin choir. Everywhere I looked I saw wild, sequestered grace. The great pines chanted like the sea, their harps of the sky touched like things celestial. And what did the music and the beauty, those extras, bring me? Passing from a state of keenest grief I came to one of quiet reconcilement—to the profound conviction that, living or dying, God will take care of us.

God seemed very near to me in that wood; the beauty of it all trembled with His grace; the music held His voice. I saw there both life and death—in the green leaves and the brown, in the standing trees and the fallen. If one is honest with himself when he asks the question, What is it that perishes? he will be obliged to answer, Everything that the eye sees. In the forest, amid those things that God provided, I came to understand that if we are to hold anything—and in times of sorrow we *must* have something to which we can cling—it must be to the unseen.

For the strength that is permanent, we have to lean on visions; for immortal hope, we have to trust, not the things that we perceive but those invisible things that our spirits affirm.

I remember walking early one July morning down a thickety path. Trees completely overarched it; but far ahead light gleamed. The path was long and straight, and terminated in a wide meadow. As I glanced upward, my eye caught sight of what I supposed to be a knot on the end of a dead limb that hung directly over the pathway; it was clearly silhouetted against the sky line ahead. In a moment something had darted over my head and had alighted on the knot. It was a hummingbird on its nest, which hung like a fairy bassinet in the lonely woodland. I looked at the nest and at the bird, with its elfin grace, its delicate sheen of brilliance, its jeweled throat. (And I thought: This whole matter of *grace*, of elegance, of delicacy and felicity of beauty is an extra. It is not necessary to have it so. But God has willed it so, because He loves us and knows our hungry hearts need this kind of beauty.)

For many years, I had an idea that nature had for man an active sympathy; but now I have changed my opinion. There seems really a superb indifference about nature. It is what lies behind nature that really has sympathy. The rose does not of itself bloom for us; but God has made it to bloom for us. Surely this beauty is not a random affair; it is too authentically a sign and symbol of love. All we know about the highest form of affection we have learned directly from God's affection for us. We not only "love Him because He first loved us," but we love one another because He teaches us how. We originate with Him; and our sublimest art is nothing but attempts to imitate the things in nature that He has created.

Whatever my religion may be worth, I feel deeply that life's extras have given it to me; and time shall not take it from me. Meditating on what we have, not merely to sustain us but to make us joyous and serene in life, I have come to so clear a consciousness of God that of all men the atheist appears to me the most pitiable and foolish. Nor have I come to this faith by roseate paths alone. I know well the Valley of the Shadow; I know the aspect of that Veil which mortal sight cannot pierce. But I know, also, that the spiritual luxuries that we so freely enjoy vindicate the faith that behind the Veil is the God of mercy and of tenderest love.

Afterword

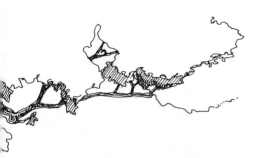

When the Yankee Band
Played Dixie
From "We Called Him Flintlock"

As a young man just out of college, I went to teach
in a preparatory school for boys in the picturesque
village of Mercersburg, Pennsylvania, situated in the
lower Cumberland Valley. The year was 1904, and at
that time there were still living in Mercersburg many
veterans of the Grand Army of the Republic.

This rural outpost had been one of the main routes
between Harrisburg and Washington, D.C., and was
an important station on the Underground Railroad,
which had helped so many slaves escape into the
North during the Civil War.

The War Between the States was still fresh in the minds of these people, I thought. Their homes had been subjected to raids by Southern troops, and only a little to the northward the important city of Chambersburg had been burned by the Confederate General McCausland.

I was the son of a Confederate colonel and I was scared, knowing that this was enemy territory and that the wounds of that cruel war were still raw and bleeding. It was not that people were not kind to me, but I felt alien and was certain that I was resented.

Also, I had the perhaps unworthy feeling that some of these old G.A.R. men had helped to devastate my homeland. Despite the fact that "I was a stranger, and they took me in," I was not happy and had a feeling of apprehension.

Yet, the school year passed without any untoward incidents, except the somewhat bewildering graciousness of the old Union soldiers toward me. We used to talk for hours. That winter one of them died, and left me his entire library.

I seemed to make many friends, but I called no one Yank, although everyone called me Johnny Reb. It occurred to me that it might be an affectionate appellation, but I was none too sure.

Throughout that first year one of my closest friends was Dr. James G. Rose, the Presbyterian minister. He was a cousin of President William McKinley. We used to play chess together, and I learned that I could lay some of my personal problems in his lap.

At length the springtime came, and on the eve of Memorial Day, still rather solitary and uncertain of my position in this community, I walked up into the ancient and beautiful cemetery that overlooks the town from a wooded hill. I have been there before to admire the primeval oaks and cedars, under which Indians must have camped before white settlers came to that region in 1750.

As I wandered through this hushed and sacred God's Acre, I saw that loving and remembering hands had already laid flowers, and had set upright little American flags on all the graves of Federal soldiers. A little apart from these I came upon three Confederate graves. I was touched to see that they, too, had been decorated with flowers, and had little American flags on them.

I thought of the beautiful lines that Francis Miles Finch, a Northerner, wrote when he saw that Federal graves had been remembered in the South by the Daughters of the Confederacy:

No more shall the war-cry sever,
    Or the winding rivers be red.
They banish our anger forever
    When they laurel the graves of our dead!
Under the sod and the dew,
    Waiting the Judgment Day,
Love and tears for the Blue,
    Tears and love for the Gray.

The cemetery in which I stood commanded a superb view of the great Cumberland Valley and of the mountains which rose on either side of it. On the eve of this hallowed Memorial Day all was at peace. Yet here great armies had marched, and here brother had slain brother.

Nature had long since done her part to heal the wounds of war, and I was to learn that human nature, though working more slowly, could come at last to beautiful reconciliation; for here before me compassionate hands had impartially covered with flowers the graves of friend and foe.

Kneeling in the twilight at the three Confederate headstones I read the names: J.W. Alban, W. H. Quaintance, and Unknown. I recognized Alban and Quaintance as Virginia names. I wondered if the families and friends of these three soldiers of the South knew what became of them.

That night I visited by good friend, Dr. Rose.

"Why, yes," he said when I told him how touched I had been to see all the soldiers' graves decorated, "we are never partial when it comes to the men who fought. I guess each side was fighting for a part of our country."

"The grave marked Unknown is that of a raider who was killed right here in our town square. Alban and Quaintance were, I believe, Virginians. They were both mortally wounded at Gettysburg. On Lee's retreat from that battlefield, a good many of his wounded men were nursed right here in the school buildings by some of our good townspeople.

"Why," he added, "Miss Alice Fenwick, I've heard, helped to nurse those two men. You must be sure to talk to her. In the face of death," he added, "people are likely to forget hatred."

As I had met Miss Alice at one of my school's social functions, it was not difficult for me to call on her. Then in her late 60s, and looking like a Dresden china doll, she received me graciously.

"Why, yes," she said, in answer to my questions about the two soldiers she had helped to nurse. "I remember the dear boys vividly—John Alban and Will Quaintance. Each one was terribly wounded, and neither one could live. You know, in those days we had so little medicine of any kind, and nearly all of our doctors were with the armies.

"I did all I could, but it was not enough. John was stoical, but Will did not want to die. Toward the end he was delirious and kept calling in the most pleading voice for Hallie. I never discovered who she was.

"And you did this just out of the goodness of your heart?" I asked.

"Why not? They were wounded and lonely and suffering. And," she went on, "we saw to it that they were given beautiful Christian burials."

I told her how deeply affected I had been when I saw that the three lonely graves in that Pennsylvania cemetery had not been neglected.

"It is the least we can do," she said. "I believe your Daughters of the Confederacy, in the Deep South, honor our boys who lie buried far from home. When a war is over," she added, "it should be over in hearts as well as on battlefields."

At that time the Richmond, Virginia, Times-Dispatch carried what was called the Confederate Column. It ran news about the old soldiers. For this paper I wrote a little article about what I had discovered in southern Pennsylvania.

A few days after it appeared, a letter came to me from Bristol, Virginia. It was signed, "Hallie (Mrs. W. H.) Quaintance." In part the letter read, "When I was a young bride, by husband disappeared on the Gettysburg campaign. From your article I am sure you have found his grave. I would like so much to come to see where he is lying."

I was not at all certain about the propriety of having

33

another Southerner come to Mercersburg, so I decided to consult my good friend, Dr. Rose. He read with grave interest my letter from Mrs. Quaintance.

"It's quite wonderful," he said. "Of course she must come and don't worry. We'll take good care of her."

Hallie Quaintance was to come by a train that reached Mercersburg late in the afternoon. I was to meet her, and I was told that she was to be entertained by Miss Alice Fenwick. The great afternoon found me reassured to some degrees, yet still apprehensive.

Since the tiny station was usually a rather desolate and deserted place I was filled with amazement when I approached it that day. The whole town was there.

There was the G.A.R. band. There were all the old G.A.R. veterans, all in uniform. There was a special carriage for the arriving guest of honor. There were scores of little flower-girls with bouquets. People filled the streets by the station, and overflowed across the tracks. I could feel the air of a loving welcome.

The train rounded a curve, chugging toward the station. At once the G.A.R. band began to play Dixie; and all of the old Federal soldiers, their caps covering their hearts, stood at attention.

I remember meeting Mrs. Quaintance, and conducting her to her carriage through a cheering and applauding throng. Then, led by the band, we all marched up to the cemetery. At every step in these proceedings I could see how carefully Dr. Rose had planned this welcome, as heartfelt as if this community had been a kingdom, and Mrs. Quaintance its reigning queen, returned from a far journey. And both in appearance and in manner she was worthy of this gracious reception.

As we drew near the three Confederate graves, in reverent silence, all the more impressive because unrehearsed, the crowd formed a great circle. Across this to the grave of the one she loved walked Hallie Quaintance. On that sacred mound she laid a wreath of flowers and knelt there briefly. When she rejoined us, her face had upon it a light of loving gratitude and spiritual peace.

For me this reception of a Confederate soldier's widow by Union veterans and their friends and families meant, in truth, the end of the Civil War. It meant Cease Firing, and the Burial of the Guns. It meant I could feel at home in what I had thought was an alien land. Indeed, I no longer wanted to be a mere Southerner. I had learned how much greater it is to be an American.

Sam Singleton, Boatman

Sam Singleton and I left home at one o'clock one
winter morning to paddle down the Santee River in
South Carolina to a place appropriately called "Tranquillity," since it is as solitary as being in the heart of
a wild delta can make it. Our plan was to drop down
ten miles or so with the ebb tide, designing to reach
at dawn the lonely hummock in the huge wasteland
that stretches mistily between the two sea-reaching
arms of the mighty river. We were to spend a few days
duck shooting at Tranquillity, and we started at a time
which would afford us sport with the morning flight.

A Southern river at night is a haunting thing, with great stars hanging like spangles in the dark pines and the ancient water oaks fringing the river shores. Wider flows the dim stream as it moves through the last reaches of the immense coastal plain. Baffling to navigate by broad daylight, the Santee at night is mysterious. And the peril of it undoubtedly was heightened by the kind of craft in which we were traveling. A dugout cypress canoe, it had as certain a tendency to roll as had its parent log, utterly lacking that virtue of stability that one relishes in a boat, especially when one is voyaging through the darkness of a huge river that seems to be wandering toward eternity.

But the stars that had been shining when we left home were soon obscured by a fog so dense that we could hardly see beyond the bow of our little boat. As we were going with the tide, we felt sure of our general direction, but when once or twice we came near looming shores, neither of us recognized the landscape as familiar. Then for an hour there was no land visible. I knew that we ought to be near our goal. But the waves that began to roll our canoe were suspiciously like sea waves. The roar of the surf that we had heard for a long time now became almost clamorous. Attempts to reach either shore were vain. The fact that the tide had now turned, or was about to turn, confused us still further. The canoe shipped water, gallons of it. The mist blinded us. There was no use blinking the truth: we were in immediate danger. I told Sam mildly that in case the canoe was swamped we must turn it over and cling to it. How can I ever forget what he said?

"Never mind, Cap'n," the humble boatman told me; *"it will be daybreak soon."*

What was there in that plight of ours on which we could certainly count? Only one thing there was: the coming of light—daybreak, sunrise! It came in time to save us, though we were really on the brink of the sea when the rosy radiance over the delta disclosed our

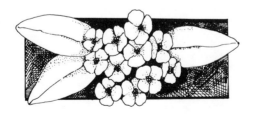

position to us. Yet it was not alone the coming of sunrise that rescued us; it was Sam's reminding me that it was *sure* to come, restoring thus my courage. And even now, after all these years, whenever the shadows are deepest and most impenetrable, I seem to hear, out of the dim celestial past, the quiet voice of Sam Singleton saying to my doubting and besieged heart, *"Never mind, Cap'n; it will be daybreak soon."*

The Compass

Regard this compass:
How veeringly the needle turns,
Yet ever northward yearns,
And at the last will come
Fatefully home.
Even so my love
Resembles
The needle; for it turns to you
And trembles.

A Song of Hope

O gallant Heart, defeated
Now gazing toward the west,
Where this day's splendor crumbles,
Disastrous and unblest, —
Look, till the deathlike darkness
By stars be glorified,
Until you see another dream
Beyond the dream that died.